Glasgow

To GRAHAM

Glasgow

Charles Jamieson

F

FRANCES LINCOLN LIMITED

PUBLISHERS

Frances Lincoln Ltd
4 Torriano Mews
Torriano Avenue
London NW5 2RZ
www.franceslincoln.com

Glasgow
Copyright © Frances Lincoln Ltd 2009
Text and photographs copyright © Charles Jamieson 2009

First Frances Lincoln edition 2009

A catalogue record for this book is available from the British Library.

ISBN 978-0-7112-2197-0

Printed and bound in Singapore

acknowledgments

One of the pleasurable aspects of working on this book has been the fact that I have met so many people, all of whom have gone out of their way to make my journey easier. I am extremely grateful for the genuine interest people have shown and for the time and effort they have put into helping me. I hope my list has included everyone. If I have missed anyone out it is not deliberate.

Dr. Denis Agnew, Malcolm S. Allan, Bae Systems, Kenneth Boyle, Calumet, Culture & Sport Glasgow, John Dale, Margaret Daly, Harvie Diamond, Claire Gemson, Glasgow City Council, Glasgow Housing Association, Glasgow Humane Society, The Glasgow School of Art, Glasgow Science Centre, Glasgow University, Peter Graham, Hampden Park Ltd, Historic Scotland, House for an Art Lover, Dorothy Johnston, Nick King, Karly Lambert, Rosy Mathieson, Jim May, Jim McDowell, Claire McGinley, Ailsa McQuat, Ken Mellin, The National Trust for Scotland, Network Rail, Martin Oestreicher, Alex Pirie, Susan Pacitti, George Parsonage MBE, The Pictures, Professor Seona Reid, Rogano Oyster Bar, John Stewart, Titan Enterprise, The Trades Hall of Glasgow, The Trades House of Glasgow, The Tall Ship at Glasgow Harbour, Allan Thomson, Jim Thomson, Rachel Whitburn, The Willow Tea Rooms, Winnie Tyrrell, Steven Winter-Griffin and T. Malcolm T. Wishart.

dedication

Finally, I dedicate this book to my parents, and to my wife Sally whose patience and support has been inexhaustible.

contents

introduction

Glasgow is a name redolent with vivid images of a colourful past: visions of magnificent ocean liners gliding into the River Clyde and being towed out to sea to begin their adventurous lives; tobacco lords whose determination and skill brought great wealth from the Americas and beyond; great comedians, actors and artists; Sir William Burrell and his collection; Victorian architecture; Alexander 'Greek' Thomson and Charles Rennie Mackintosh. Glasgow Is made up of layer upon layer of people, places, happenings and history.

The Glasgow we have today is the result of over a thousand years of struggle for survival; struggle to make itself heard, to overcome the hardships of day to day life, to strike out and succeed in trade and industry, bringing wealth to the city whilst trying to contain and look after its growing population.

It is this abIlity to survIve, this determination in the face of gritty reality which gives the people of Glasgow their humanity and their humour.

So what of Glasgow now? Having pulled itself from the depths of post war, post industrial depression it stands a successful, wealthy, handsome city – a city, however, still in the throes of physical change. The regeneration that started after the war is ongoing. Huge areas have been demolished and a great new modern face is being built. Glasgow is now a financial and business centre, a centre for tourism, the arts, sport and all the things the modern economy demands of it.

Cities, like people, must adapt to survive. Economic pressures, local, national and international, that force change are what shape our cities and our lives. At one end of the scale the wider global economy determines the way the city stretches itself in order to bring in trade and business and the necessary finance in order to thrive, and at the other end, smaller local economies and the way they are handled are the deciding factors on how many who inhabit the city live.

ABOVE
Statue of Thomas Graham in George Square

OPPOSITE
The bird, the fish, the bell and the tree (elements of Glasgow's coat of arms) encompassed in a lamppost shaped as a Bishop's crook symbolising the closeness of the Church and the city

We have in Glasgow a wide, deep river spanned by many bridges with more being built. Shipbuilding within city boundaries is limited to the Bae Systems yard in Govan who supply ships to the world's navies. New, sometimes iconic buildings are emerging on its banks and once busy docks. So too are areas of housing and recreation. Plans to open the river up for public use with riverside walks already in place promise great things for this once thriving industrial basin. Tourist attractions such as the Science Centre with its 127 metre high tower (the tallest free-standing structure in Scotland) and the hugely awaited Riverside Museum designed by Zaha Hadid are turning areas of the river into exciting focal points for residents and tourists alike.

It is easy to walk along the river and admire it in all its majesty without casting a thought as to its history. To look at its bridges without wondering how they came into being. To walk through the Victorian centre of the city and take its buildings for granted.

This book is a visual celebration of Glasgow with a text that hopefully throws some light on this fertile, complicated and much loved city.

OPPOSITE TOP
The Bae shipyard in Govan

OPPOSITE CENTRE
The Albert Bridge (1871)

OPPOSITE BELOW
The weir by Glasgow Green

RIGHT
The Glasgow Tower, Science
Centre and Imax Cinema on
Princes Dock

history

It seems only sensible to take a brief historical look at the city. This is a loose time line and it has made me see Glasgow in a new light. This page and three following chapters (the cathedral, trade and the development of the city, and the city) will work through the historical time line.

In its early life, the land that Glasgow is built upon was shaped by glacial activity. Advancing, retreating and melting glaciers deposited boulder clay which formed Glasgow's hills (known as drumlins), some of which were moulded by the emerging river which was extremely deep, and much of what we now know as Glasgow would have been under water.

When man first settled at the point which is now the city centre the river had become much shallower, often less than two feet deep in places. Rich with salmon and herring, it provided an easily obtainable food source. The depth of the water meant that salmon traps could be laid without difficulty. Nearby, the plains and hill country were excellent for hunting. Wild cattle, bears, red deer, wolves and other animals were all to be found, giving not only a food supply but also animal products: sinews, furs and bones. Local clay was good for making pots. All that was needed to sustain life was readily available.

These early settlements were more often than not on coastlines or by rivers as the interior tended to be difficult, often impenetrable, terrain. Canoes, fashioned from tree trunks gave easy access to other areas and communities. In places the river was easy enough to ford, indeed the Romans used this point to cross on foot after they had advanced into Scotland in AD 80.

LEFT
Views from the Glasgow Tower with
the Clyde Auditorium on the left and
the BBC on the right

11

the cathedral

Around AD 560 Glasgow began its long journey as a religious centre with the arrival of St Kentigern (better known as St Mungo) from Culross in Fife. He established a church by the Molendinar Burn. Today the cathedral sits close by but whether it is on the exact spot that St Kentigern built his church is debatable.

Historical records of early Glasgow and its surrounding areas are a little thin on the ground but in the early twelfth century things begin to change with the founding of the Glasgow diocese. It is through the Bishops of Glasgow, whose interests were, by necessity, both ecclesiastical and secular, that we have the beginnings of the documentation of every day life, albeit that many of the early records are not wholly reliable. At the time when a cathedral was commissioned Glasgow was a predominantly ecclesiastical and agricultural town in a country divided and ruled over by the brothers Alexander (in the Highlands) and David (in the Lowlands). This had been the case since 1107 but with Alexander's death in 1124 the country was reunited under King David.

When Bishop John took office sometime before 1118, plans were drawn up to provide a cathedral. David was a great supporter, after all it was he who appointed John as Bishop. The erection of the early cathedral was begun prior to 1124. The cathedral was dedicated in July 1136 in the presence of King David though in all probability it was not yet completed. Commonly known as Bishop John's Cathedral, it was in the Norman style and one can imagine the impact it made. In the late twelfth century Bishop Jocelin was overseeing new building works when a fire caused serious damage. A second dedication took place in 1197 though once again work remained unfinished.

Successive Bishops played their part in construction but it is thought that Bishop William De Bondington in the mid-thirteenth century started the work that would eventually transform the building into the Gothic cathedral we have today but it was to be a long process. Inspiration seems to have come from both an English design of the twelfth century and adaptations of that design by Cistercian monks. Having said that, the building was in no way completed on these plans alone, and through time modifications and extensions were added. There were also repairs which in themselves brought about change (in one case, repairs were due to the building being struck by lightning).

The importance of the existence of the cathedral is two fold. On the one hand it shows the influence that Glasgow had as a religious centre and that in turn helped the growth of the burgh on the banks of the Clyde that eventually became the great city of today. Whilst the river would undoubtedly have retained a community on its banks, it was the power of the church and the support of the crown that allowed Glasgow to flourish where others did not.

The cathedral itself is now protected by Historic Scotland who watch over this great building which is the only one on mainland Scotland to have survived unscathed through the Reformation.

ABOVE TOP
Looking down the nave

ABOVE
The Blackadder Aisle

OPPOSITE
Glasgow Cathedral

the necropolis

The Necropolis, which sits on the hill behind the cathedral, is the first of four such cemeteries but is without doubt the most impressive. It opened in 1833 having been built by the Trustees of the Merchant's House who for many years had been caring for this hillside which was so popular for its views across the city and its monument to John Knox.

A massive rise in Glasgow's population from some 83,000 in 1800 to something in the region of 200,000 by 1830 created a number of problems. The increased pressure on the river and the lack of clean drinking water brought both cholera and typhoid epidemics. Conditions in overcrowded church graveyards did not help and the need for organised cemeteries became apparent. The Trustees laid out plans for the Necropolis as somewhere for the most eminent citizens of Glasgow to be laid to rest.

Distinguished architects such as Alexander 'Greek' Thomson designed many of the tombs and monuments and the end result is this superb Victorian cemetery.

BELOW
Looking towards the Templeton Carpet Factory building from the Necropolis

OPPOSITE
The Necropolis with the John Knox Monument to the right of centre

trade and the development of the city

From the earliest times Glasgow has traded. At first with near neighbours and as time progressed and society developed Glasgow looked further afield with both imports and exports. With travel across land so difficult, the river provided the perfect passageway. Consequently the river has always been a hotbed of controversy regarding rights of usage. At first it was ownership of rights to fish particular parts of the river and the use of the river banks themselves. Rights to take boats through certain stretches of water. Rights to build landing points and piers. There was much rivalry along the river bank and charges were levied for all sorts of activities all the way down to the coast. Being so far inland and existing by shallow waters, Glasgow's survival depended on creating relationships with neighbours like Rutherglen and Renfrew who were older, more established burghs, and also with ports further down river where larger ships could dock. In this age of great rivalry it would have been easy for these burghs to have blocked Glasgow and stifled its development were it not for the influence the town held from the twelfth century onwards. (Despite this, in years to come, Renfrew and Rutherglen were often accused of obstructing the free entrance of goods to Glasgow's market.)

In order to bring cargoes from down river to Glasgow, small boats known as lighters would make their way to Dumbarton, Greenock, Irvine and Ayr, load up and make their way back. This was an expensive operation. Traders and merchants paid heavily for the right to operate in this way. Fees to access the ports were high. It was also slow and cumbersome. There were stretches of river where there was little wind and if the tides were especially low, as often happened, the lighters were unable to access Glasgow itself, sometimes for weeks on end.

At the time when it was becoming easier to transport goods on land, the river, though relatively easy to cross at low tide on foot, was impossible with a horse and cart. So in 1284 or 1285 Glasgow built a wooden bridge across the Clyde to

Govan. (Today Victoria Bridge sits on the same spot.) This aided the movement of goods and enhanced the status of the town. That first bridge was replaced by a stone bridge in 1345, known as Bishop Rae's Bridge.

In 1451 a Papal bull was issued for the establishment of a university, an important step for Glasgow and the beginnings of one of the oldest universities in Europe. The first classes were held in the cathedral's lower church.

By 1610 the population had risen to 7,644 (this can be seen in the excellent time line in the museum at the Trades Hall in Glassford Street).

ABOVE
The Tall Ship *Glenlee* at Glasgow Harbour is one of the few sailing ships built on the Clyde that is still afloat

OPPOSITE
The Titan crane in Clydebank

LEFT
Glasgow has a history of inner city clocks, this one was designed by the artist Charles Anderson

BELOW LEFT
Detail in West George Street

OPPOSITE
The Ca d'Oro building (1872) at the corner of Union Street and Gordon Street

In 1611 James VI granted a charter making Glasgow a Royal burgh. By this time there are some names we can now recognise; the High Street, Trongate and Gallowgate. Most of the buildings would stretch from the cathedral, down the High Street to the Tolbooth and on to the river.

For some time then, the town had had a rising population which in turn created an unstoppable course of development and the basis of the city we have today. As in all intensely populated areas the job of looking after the town and its population became ever more complicated. These days the Council meets in George Square but back in the fifteenth century a tolbooth on the corner of the High Street served as a meeting place. Over the next 400 years they were to move several times, to the Trongate in 1735, Jail Square in 1814 and twice more before moving into the City Chambers which were completed in 1888.

One of the great success stories of early Glasgow is that of the salmon fishers who not only supplied food locally but also traded salted fish in barrels. Often the rights to fish were conveyed along with houses in the burgh. Salmon fishers' huts were a common sight along the banks of the river and salmon fishing was one of Glasgow's most important industries, though by the seventeenth century other industries had been established. Cloth factories in Drygate, coal pits in the Gorbals and candle factories. 1630 saw the first letter printing press. This was a growing and developing environment which attracted more and more people into the town. One of the centres of the salmon industry at the westernmost part of Glasgow was Fishergate, which from the sixteenth century was beside a well, known as the Stock Well: now the bottom of Stockwell Street.

Despite the growing industry and trade, Glasgow suffered several setbacks. In 1649 the plague devastated the town. Following that was the great fire of 1652 which destroyed almost a third of existing buildings. Most houses were constructed from wood and many bore thatched roofs. Even those built with stone were usually only stone on the first floor and timber thereafter (some had wooden frontages with circular holes cut for an easy view of the street). Fire was able to spread rapidly. This catastrophic fire left about a thousand families homeless. A collection was made across the kingdom and grants given for reconstruction.

In 1660 changes were made to the English Navigation Ordinance and the English Navigation Act was created. The main thrust of the Navigation Ordinance had been that English trade should be carried out in English vessels only. The new Navigation Act made it clear that all trade with the Indies and Americas should be with English and Welsh vessels, thus preventing the Scots from having a share of this opening market. This caused much disquiet as the Clyde had become an important trading river. (It also paved the way for the Act of Union in 1707 which would open up trade to the

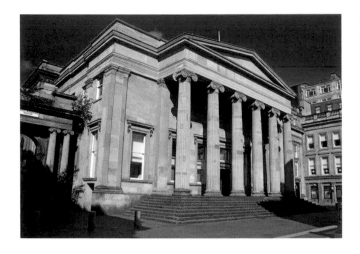

ABOVE LEFT
Royal Exchange Square

ABOVE RIGHT
Virginia Court

OPPOSITE
Trinity College building

Indies and Americas to the Scots. Scottish merchants could see the benefits of the Union and it made sense despite some upset at the idea of a union with England from the general populace.)

In 1667 fire struck once again destroying 136 houses and shops. The heat was so intense at the Cross that the clock in the Tolbooth caught fire and prisoners had to be released lest they perish. Six or seven hundred families were affected and the Council decided that all buildings should from then on be made of stone. This is minuted in Council records though it would seem that it was largely ignored.

In 1684 yet another fire in Gallowgate was prevented from spreading by the use of wet hides laid across thatched roofs and hung down the sides of buildings.

By the end of the seventeenth century and faced with the fact that in this time of increasing trade the river was too shallow to allow ships to reach Glasgow, the decision was made to build a new port relatively close by. Newport consisted of a harbour, a graving (dry dock) and a group of houses. No one trading from Glasgow could load or unload at any other port and if they did so they would face heavy fines. There was still a high percentage of trade through other ports but Newport gave Glasgow a degree of independence. Newport thrived and in time was renamed Port Glasgow.

The use of seafaring vessels increased dramatically and the nearby ports of Greenock and Port Glasgow were of enormous importance in helping Glasgow become an international trade centre. The population by 1740 had reached 17,043 but both prosperity and the political problems within Scotland caused it to increase dramatically so that by 1782 it was 42,000. (The eighteenth century saw great unrest within Scotland, with the Jacobite rebellions, Culloden and the destruction of the Clan system.)

The eighteenth century also saw trade increase with the English colonies in America and the tobacco trade brought great wealth, peaking in 1772. In the latter part of the century the Merchant City was established and elegant mansions were built for wealthy traders and merchants. The main trades were the importation of tobacco and ginger and exporting linens, ironware, glass and leather. However, trading in tobacco meant profiting from the slave trade. This is something that the city is now having to come to terms with. The bicentenary of the abolishment of the slave trade in 2007 happened also to be the tercentenary of the Act of Union which gave Scotland the right to trade with the West Indies. Although it is unlikely that the city actually took part in the shipping of slaves from Africa to the West Indies and America it certainly benefited hugely from the profits.

The tobacco lords became the city's first millionaires and their names echo throughout the city to this day... Ingram, Cochrane, Glassford, Buchanan and Dunlop. So too do the place names they traded with: Jamaica, Virginia, Tobago and Kingston.

In the 1770s, the American War of Independence gave the Americans the right to trade with anyone rather than having to trade solely with Great Britain. This affected Glasgow's part in the tobacco trade but by that time it was well established as a trading centre and simply changed it's focus to importing cotton and other goods. This brought about a move towards the textile industries and the manufacture of cotton goods. In 1816, a sailing ship, the *Earl of Buckingham*, was the first ship to sail directly from the Clyde to India.

The expansion of the population through the eighteenth and into the nineteenth century brought with it overcrowding and slum conditions. The river was still the main source of drinking water as well as providing washing facilities, water for factories and a place to dump sewage. Disease was inevitable and cholera and typhoid epidemics were regular occurrences. In the early nineteenth century these epidemics increased in numbers.

The major changes to the river began in the nineteenth century as engineering developed. There were many projects

over many years overseen by some of the great pioneers of engineering. Thomas Telford advised on how to improve access to the city. John Rennie was responsible for docks being built on both banks of the river at the Broomielaw.

In order to deepen and widen the river, the Clyde was subject to blasting, excavating and dredging to create a basin suitable for the planned expansion.

New docks were built to allow for more trade and the beginning of shipbuilding. Though this made way for massive regeneration it also spelled the beginning of the end for the salmon industry. The river, once so suited to the salmon, was changing and the pollution from the many cloth factories, printers and other works was having a profound effect. The emergence of heavy industry would add greatly to that pollution and the salmon eventually disappeared. Many areas were changed forever as the docks were constructed, something that we can sympathise with today as we see areas of the city being flattened as part of the current regeneration programme. As always, the regeneration of the city also meant architectural sacrifice. We may never know exactly what was lost but the process is part and parcel of the survival of the city.

Throughout the nineteenth century Glasgow flourished despite its problems. It was, after all, ideally situated for trade and the wealth that trade could bring drove Glasgow forwards. The relationship between the Merchants and the Trades Guilds (which had seen a period of disagreement over

ABOVE LEFT
Detail of carving in Gordon Street

ABOVE RIGHT
The Tobacco Merchant's House,
Miller Street

RIGHT
Virginia Place

OPPOSITE
The Trades Hall of Glasgow

their status in terms of the towns Council in the seventeenth century) had become one of a shared vision and pride. In the latter part of the century heavy industry brought a second wave of great wealth and with it a massive amount of building. Glasgow was to become *the* Victorian city. The city's history of expansion and heavy industry is a microcosm of the history of the Industrial Revolution. Of all the industries Glasgow boasted, the one that outstripped all the rest was shipbuilding though the building of locomotives and steam engines came a close second. Glasgow became the greatest centre of shipbuilding in the world and that took the city comfortably into the twentieth century, with the industry at it's peak just prior to the First World War in 1914. At this point Glasgow was known as the second city of the Empire. It was the fourth largest city in the world and was riding high.

From this point until the end of the First World War in 1919 shipbuilding reached its zenith though no one knew it at the time. After the war there was an international slump and Glasgow and the Clyde did not really recover until the late

thirties and celebrated the possible and hoped for future with the Empire Exhibition in 1938.

Then came the Second World War. Fortunately the city of Glasgow itself escaped the bombing but its close neighbour Clydebank suffered terribly in the Clydebank Blitz. The real heart of shipbuilding was in Clydebank. Glasgow as a city profited from the industry and indeed had several shipyards itself but it was Clydebank, further down the river where it was wider and deeper, that boasted the biggest yards. Consequently it was Clydebank that was targeted by the Luftwaffe. The idea had been to take out the heavy industry that lay alongside the river. The first wave of planes were to drop incendiaries which would guide the bombers to their targets. They planned to use the river as their marker and drop the incendiaries alongside in the industrial areas but a terrible mistake made this one of the great disasters of the war for Scotland. It had been raining and the Luftwaffe pilots mistook the moonlight reflecting off the wide main road that ran between the industrial area and the residential area as

the river itself and dropped their devices in what they thought was the industrial part. In fact they dropped the incendiaries in the residential areas and the waves of bombers that followed systematically destroyed Clydebank's housing. Over two thousand died, thousands more were rendered homeless. The stories of tragedy and heroism from the Blitz are as alive and deeply felt today as they were then.

It was after the Second World War that the decline in heavy industry really began. Glasgow Corporation recognised that the city faced an uncertain future in a changing world and started to make the plans that would eventually lead to the great regeneration programme that the city has been undergoing for the last half century.

Since the sixties we have witnessed regeneration on an unparalleled scale in the city. Recently the river has been the centre of this with the creation of foot and road bridges as well as walkways, which herald a new future as a recreational area for this much loved stretch of water. One new bridge is the Clyde Arc known affectionately as 'Squinty Bridge'

which brings traffic into the newly developed south side which houses the Science Centre, the BBC and Scottish Television.

Over on the north bank the Finnieston crane (Clyde Navigation Trusts crane number 7), the largest crane within city limits, stands as a reminder of the busy working place the river once was. Built in 1931, this 175 ton steel structure was used to move the heaviest loads on and off ships. Many of the great steam trains built here found themselves being loaded onto ships by the Finnieston crane as they started their journeys abroad. Further down river at Clydebank on the site that once housed John Brown's shipyard, the gigantic Titan crane has also been preserved and towers over the riverside and the new Clydebank College. Newly fitted with a lift and a viewing platform, this 150 foot cantilever crane built in 1907 sits at the side of the old fitting basin. It was used to lower engines and boilers into great ships such as the *Lusitania*, the *Britannia* and the QE2.

the city

Glasgow is blessed with many fine buildings often inspired by travel and by movements such as Art Nouveau, Art Deco, Modernism and Classicism. Examples of influence from ancient cultures across the world are to be found in the city. Glasgow has, in turn, inspired those to whom it looks, especially Chicago.

This huge architectural potpourri lives in one harmonious melting pot and is testimony to an appetite for travel and discovery shared by all Scots. These many styles, written in stone, tell the story of Glasgow's architects, their travels and love of historical and foreign architecture and of the great wealth that allowed them to indulge their passions. Glasgow has many celebrated architects who have helped create this rich heritage but two of them stand above all the others: Charles Rennie Mackintosh and Alexander 'Greek' Thomson. Both brought to the city large portfolios of astonishing works and the city is all the richer for them. Although most of their works have survived, some sadly have not.

In Glasgow we are lucky that so many great buildings have been erected and given us so much pleasure. The city is not, however, standing still in architectural terms. Glasgow continues to employ great architects to create buildings that will hopefully become as iconic as their predecessors. Sir Norman Foster, Zaha Hadid and others are adding to the city's collection.

The history of cities and their development provide the skeleton upon which the structure of a city will hang. The granting of the right to build a cathedral and the choosing of a site for that cathedral created one of the first real pieces of town planning that have dictated the layout of the city as we know it today.

The erection of the early cathedral was begun prior to

LEFT
The Weir, the Albert Bridge and
the city centre

1124. Its situation, set back from the river, created the need for the High Street to develop into an important thoroughfare as it ran down to what is now the Tolbooth and the various dwellings that were very much the centre of the town. The cathedral seems to anchor the city to its historical roots.

Some of the earliest stone buildings in Glasgow were built around the cathedral and down the High Street. Very little remains apart from Provand's Lordship, which is the oldest house in the city.

The truly great period of building ran through the late eighteenth, nineteenth and early twentieth century. Glasgow had made a fortune, firstly from the tobacco trade and trade with the Indies in the eighteenth century, then with heavy industry in the latter half of the nineteenth century and into the twentieth century.

This long period of wealth creation was when the great stone buildings were built and the city centre eventually took shape. Nearly all of the early merchants' houses that made up the eighteenth century Merchant City are no longer there but one still exists in Miller Street somewhat sandwiched between newer less interesting buildings. The Tobacco Merchant's House at number 42 is, rather fittingly, now the home of the Glasgow Buildings Preservation Trust who help to maintain many of the city's buildings and also organise the Glasgow Doors Open Day during which a number of great buildings not normally accessible to the public open their doors.

ABOVE
Provand's Lordship (1471), the oldest house in Glasgow

OPPOSITE
Detail in Bothwell Street

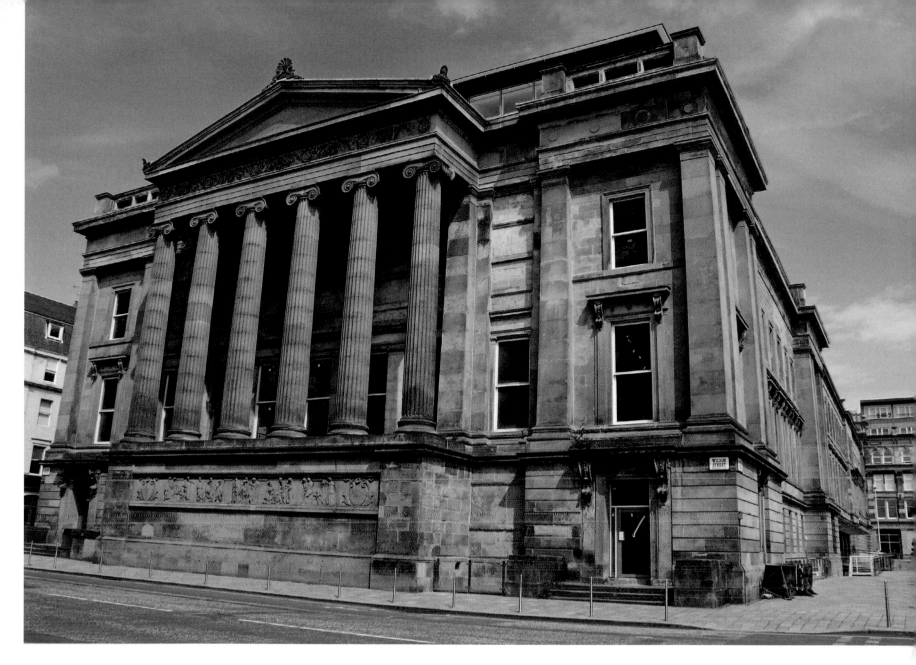

ABOVE
Former City and County buildings,
Wilson Street

OPPOSITE
St George's Church, Buchanan
Street

ABOVE
The Glasgow Gallery of Modern Art
in Exchange Square

ABOVE
Statue of the Duke of Wellington, by
Baron Carlo Marochetti, in front of
the Glasgow Gallery of Modern Art

OPPOSITE
The Tolbooth Steeple (c.1626)

RIGHT
St Andrew's Parish Church,
St Andrew's Square

glasgow central station

OPPOSITE and TOP RIGHT
Central Station

BOTTOM RIGHT
Central Hotel (1883) from where
John Logie Baird made history by
transmitting the first image thus
paving the way for television

Toward the end of the nineteenth century, Glasgow made the decision to build Central Station in the city centre. Previously, passengers travelled from Bridge Street (1840), the first passenger terminus in the city, which was across the river from the city centre itself, and from the Glebe Street terminal. There was also a network of railways linked to warehouses, grain mills and transport depots whose primary purpose was the movement of goods to the city to keep the population fed and clothed and to provide all necessary materials for the continuation of life in an ever expanding and more demanding city.

By the 1870s Bridge Street had become a busy through station so there was a real need to create a new station that would serve as a terminus. The decision to build across the river and into the city centre meant uprooting the population of Grahamston and tearing down what had been a thriving village since at least the seventeenth century. However, in order to create the new terminus, large areas of land had to be cleared to allow for the station itself, the tracks and the bridge. The new Central Station opened in 1879.

By the end of the century the level of demand on the station was such that it had to be radically expanded. This included the building of a new bridge over the river to accommodate the increased number of tracks. At the same time, due to its popularity, Central Hotel was enlarged. Work began in 1901 and ran for five years through all of which the station remained operational.

The station has been constantly updated throughout the years taking in its stride changes from steam to diesel to electricity. New signalling systems, new ticketing systems, new lines, dealing with new railway companies, new transport authorities and the changing needs of an ever demanding public.

In 1984 major works began to revitalise the station, the two most significant features being the laying of polished white tile over the entire concourse and the change from

the old hand operated indicator boards to the new electronic system. For three years, starting in 1997, over six acres of roof glazing were refurbished. In 2004 Central Station was awarded a Europa Nostra Award.

LEFT
The City Chambers, the Jubilee
Pediment

OPPOSITE
The City Chambers and Cenotaph
in George Square

glasgow city chambers

The City Chambers is one of the great features of Glasgow. Sitting proudly beside George Square, this magnificent building has all the majesty one expects in a city dominated by Victorian grandeur.

The building was designed by Paisley-born William Young who entered his design into a competition for purpose built council offices in the early 1880s. This was the second round of competition, the first round having failed to find a design that incorporated enough sculpture.

This was an interesting period as the city's wealth had been increasing substantially for over a century and with it came confidence and the desire to show the world through its architecture that Glasgow was able to compete with the best of them. There were already a number of fine buildings standing in the city so this one really had to make its presence felt. Ornate classical was the order of the day and William Young's design was a triumph of decoration and classical opulence. Building began in 1883 with the foundation stone being laid by the Lord Provost in the October.

The city had been in need of a permanent home for its Council. As the city had expanded over the centuries so too had the council and its responsibilities. They had found themselves in various homes over the years moving to Wilson Street in 1844 and then Ingram Street in 1874 before settling into the City Chambers upon its completion.

The inauguration ceremony was performed by Queen Victoria in 1888 despite the fact that the buildings interiors were unfinished. This came about because the Queen was visiting the International Exhibition in Kelvingrove Park and the city took advantage of her presence. The building was opened in September 1889 attracting hundreds of thousands of visitors in the first weeks.

The building itself is made of granite with sandstone statues and reliefs. The interiors boast ornate mosaics, coloured granites and marbles, alabaster and a stained glass dome.

ABOVE LEFT
Looking down from the Upper
Gallery

ABOVE RIGHT
The Upper Gallery

OPPOSITE
Interior staircase, the City
Chambers

the university of glasgow

Glasgow was granted the right to have a university by means of a Papal bull (lead seal) in 1451 thus creating the second university in Scotland, the other being founded at St Andrews in 1410. This was an important step for Glasgow and created one of the oldest universities in Europe and the fourth oldest in the United Kingdom.

The Papul bull gave Bishop William Turbull the authorisation he needed to set the university in motion. At first, classes were held in the chapterhouse of the cathedral.

In 1460 the university moved to a building in the High Street. For the next 400 years this was to be its home. Courtyards, gardens and a handsome clocktower were the setting for the growth of learning in the city. In 1871 the university moved to its present home in Gilmorehill. Sadly, the building in the High Street was demolished which was a great loss to the city. However, one lodge and the Lion and Unicorn staircase were taken and incorporated into the new campus. The new university which overlooks the River Kelvin and Kelvingrove Art Gallery and Museum, was designed by Sir George Gilbert Scott. His son, Sir John Aldred Scott, added the spire. Renowned as one of the world's great universities and famed for its research capabilities, it has over 20,000 students and a huge staff.

In 2007/08 it was named *Sunday Times* Scottish University of the Year.

RIGHT
The University of Glasgow

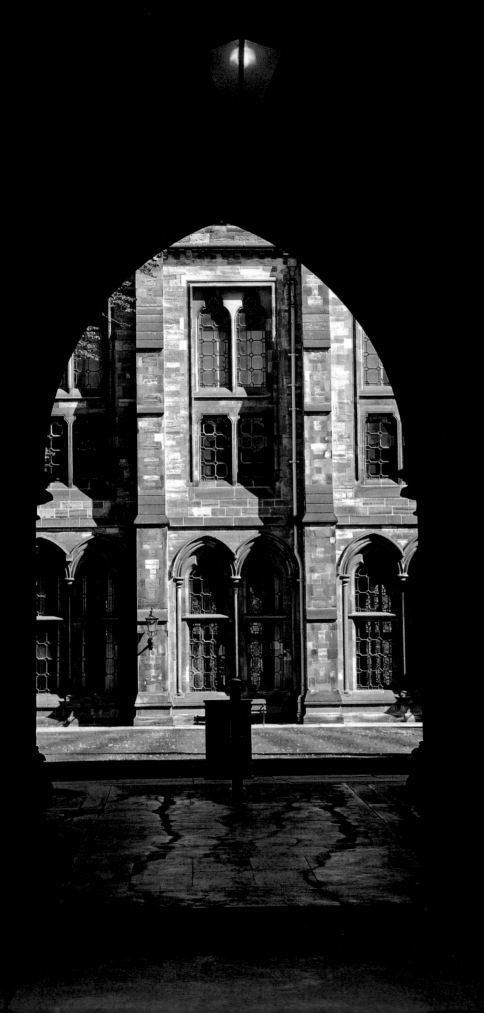

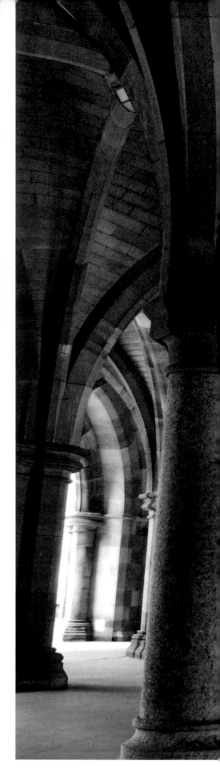

ABOVE
The undercroft of the Bute Hall, the
University of Glasgow

LEFT
Looking into the East Quadrangle,
the University of Glasgow

alexander 'greek' thomson

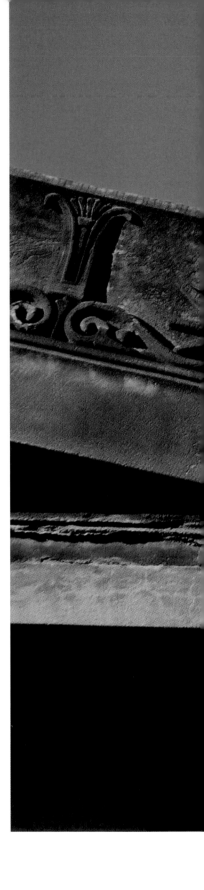

Born in Balfron in Stirlingshire in 1817 and one of twelve children, Alexander Thomson was to become the first truly great architect in Glasgow. He never travelled but gained inspiration through books on the architectural styles of the world, concentrating on classical Greek and Egyptian.

He set up a practice with his brother George in the late 1850s that became hugely popular and successful. His work is mainly to be found within Glasgow but there are examples across Scotland. The variety of buildings is impressive, including villas, terraces, tenements, warehouses and churches for which many say he is best known.

holmwood house

Owned by the National Trust for Scotland who have been renovating Holmwood for some years, it is a fine, if not the best example, of a 'Greek' Thomson house. The renovation work by the Trust has uncovered much of the original decoration and though patchy in places it shows how magnificent Holmwood must have been when new.

Holmwood House in Cathcart was built between 1856 and 1858 for one James Coupar who, with his brother, owned paper mills by the River Cart. After the Second World War Holmwood House became a convent.

Thomson is well known for creating complex designs and both the Knowe and Holmwood are similar in the way they have been put together, though Holmwood is considerably larger and of the two its design is the more harmonious.

A long wall joins the house to what used to be a stable block but is now used as accommodation that can be rented.

ABOVE
Detail of the St Vincent Street
Church

LEFT
Holmwood House, the National
Trust for Scotland

49

ABOVE
Bay window interior, Holmwood
House

RIGHT
Holmwood House

ABOVE
Detail exterior stonework,
Holmwood House

RIGHT
Detail dining room wall,
Holmwood House

the knowe

Designed in 1850 and built in 1853, the Knowe is said to be the first Italianate villa built in Glasgow. It was extended in 1858. As a building it displays many of the ideas that Thomson would develop in the years to come. It is closely linked to Holmwood House and recognised as the inspiration for Holmwood.

The Knowe sits on a plot of land on the corner of Albert Drive and Shields Road with impressive gateways leading to the house and surrounding flats. The house is now split into three residences but still retains its character and is in excellent condition.

The interiors are sumptuous and the many unusual stained glass windows add to the beauty of the building.

ABOVE
The Knowe

OPPOSITE LEFT
St Vincent Street Church

OPPOSITE RIGHT
Caledonian Road Church

charles rennie mackintosh

Charles Rennie Mackintosh (1868–1928) was one of eleven children. Born and brought up in Glasgow, it is impossible to describe Mackintosh solely as an architect. He was also an artist and designer creating in a variety of mediums and producing some of the most exciting work of his day. His love of Art Nouveau and Japanese design melded together to make a unique visual language. His was not an easy life. His work caused some controversy and was a far cry from the heavy Victorian architecture to which Glasgow had become accustomed. He was not celebrated as an artist in his home country though he was recognised in Europe. After training at art school in Glasgow, he joined the firm of Honeyman and Keppie who gave him a thorough grounding in the practice of architecture.

In 1900 he married the artist Margaret Macdonald and they often collaborated on projects.

His true genius was recognised after his death and Glasgow is fortunate to be home to some of his greatest architectural achievements.

glasgow school of art

Recognised as Mackintosh's masterpiece, the Glasgow School of Art broke the architectural expectations of Victorian Glasgow. For years the city had celebrated its status as the Victorian city with ever more elaborate buildings, so when a competition was announced in 1896 for the design of a new art school by the school's Governors and its Director 'Fra' Newbery, people no doubt assumed that a building based on classical lines and adorned with sculptures would be constructed to fit in with the current trend. However the budget available for this building was remarkably low in comparison with the budgets that had gone before, and that in itself attracted much comment. The Governors let it be known that they were looking for a 'plain' building, one that would be practical.

OPPOSITE
Library, Glasgow School of Art

RIGHT
Exterior of Glasgow School of Art

Mackintosh worked at the time for the architects Honeyman and Keppie. It was only a few years since he had left art school and he held a very junior position. The low budget involved, the tricky site at the top of the hill and the restraints of the brief all worked in Mackintosh's favour as the firm decided that this project was one that Mackintosh should be given a chance to prove himself on. And prove himself he did. His design was unveiled as the winning one in 1897. It was an extremely courageous decision by the judges though it was greeted with incredulity from just about everyone else.

We look at the School of Art now and see the most beautifully balanced decoration that works with the building rather than having been simply stuck on. However, at the time opinions were very different. The population had grown used to highly ornate buildings and this was anything but. They were used to historically classical references and this had none, at least none that they recognised.

Though Mackintosh, like other architects, had drawn upon foreign influences, bringing in some European Art Nouveau and designs based upon Japanese heraldry in the ironwork, he had, more than anything else, designed a practical building where the decoration paid homage to the buildings use. The end result is that the decoration and the building meld together harmoniously.

The end of the nineteenth and beginning of the twentieth centuries was the beginning of a time of change. A change compounded by the First World War when society itself was thrown into a new reality. Mackintosh helped herald that change and those that chose his design played their part.

As a practical art school building it was, and still is, extremely successful. The painting studios with their enormous windows give an even uninterrupted north light. The decorative ironwork on the outside of the windows does not interfere at all. The main gallery, lit from above and emphasising those great wooden beams is a superb space for displaying art. The side stairways are perfect for the movement of large numbers of students through the building. The decoration in these spaces is economic and simple with moments of intense detail carved above doors and stained glass in the doors themselves, iron beam ends, clocks and gridded ironwork. The showpiece in the building is the library which is a masterpiece of structural design.

LEFT TOP
East finial, Glasgow School of Art

LEFT CENTRE AND BELOW
Wall decoration in side staircase

RIGHT
Roof beam in the museum, first floor, Glasgow School of Art

LEFT TOP
First floor corridor looking towards the library

LEFT BELOW
The loggia

OPPOSITE TOP
Sign above the front entrance

OPPOSITE BELOW
Left hand entrance door

willow tea rooms

When Mackintosh designed the Willow Tea Rooms (1903–4) for Miss Cranston in an already existing row of buildings, he simplified the facade and painted it white and it remains so to this day. The decorative ironwork holding the signage symbolises the city's coat of arms with the bird, the fish, the bell and the tree. Once again the interior is designed to the last detail. Mackintosh and his wife Margaret collaborated in designing everything: chairs, tables, light fittings, carpets, curtains and even the menus. It is quite something that this tea room has survived for more than a century and is still in use. In that time it has changed hands, changed names and undergone restoration by Keppie Henderson Architects prior to being reopened once again as the Willow Tea Rooms in 1983. The ground floor of the building now houses Henderson's the Jewellers.

The main tea room, the Gallery, is based upon Japanese themes emphasising an ordered, uncomplicated design. The whole area has a diffused soft light due to gauze being stretched across the ceiling and is a peaceful place to enjoy a cup of tea with friends.

Upstairs in the Room De Luxe, Mackintosh uses a rose motif throughout in silver, pinks and greys. Ornate stained glass doors lead you in to the room with decorative mirrors on the walls and lead panelled windows. There is a panel designed by Margaret on one side and the room is hung with beautiful light fittings.

Upstairs again is the Billiard Room which is mostly blue and black and which is used as a display area with a few pieces of Mackintosh furniture and other interesting artefacts. Of especial interest are the light fittings, the windows and window catches.

ABOVE LEFT
Ironwork sign alluding to Glasgow's coat of arms

ABOVE RIGHT
The Billiard Room

OPPOSITE
The Room De Luxe

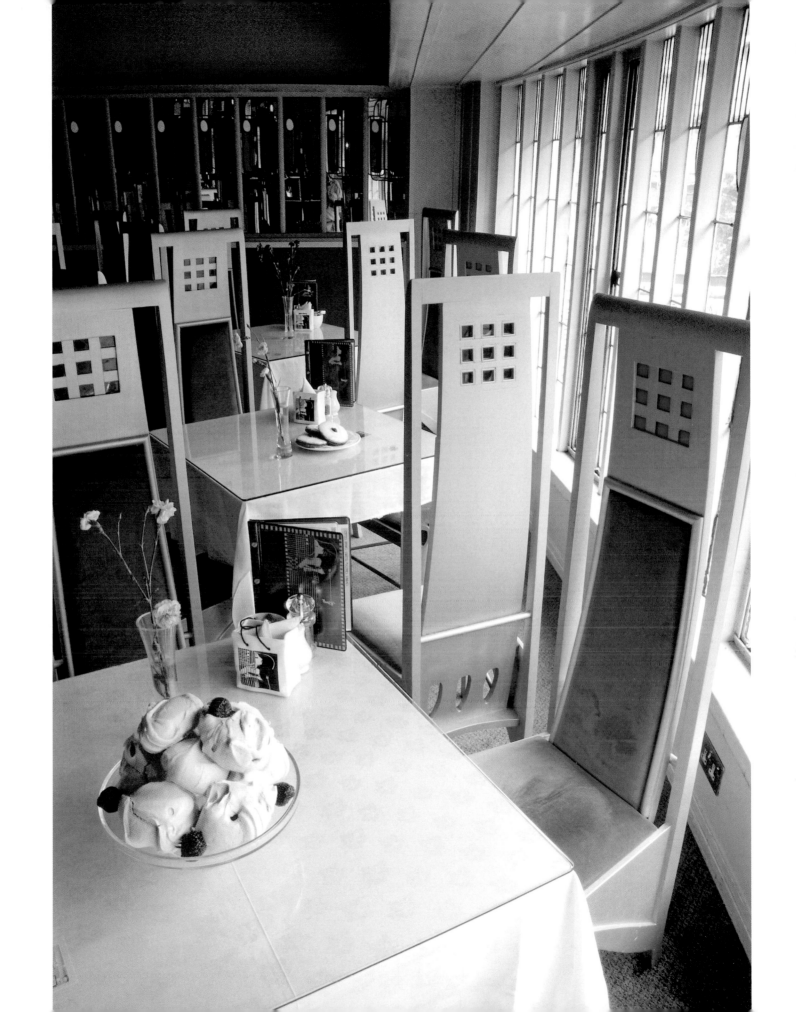

scotland street school

This period was the most prolific for Mackintosh and indeed the most varied in terms of commissions, though Scotland Street School was to be his last commission in Glasgow itself. The School was designed in 1903 and built between 1904 and 1906 when it opened. There was no budget for interior decoration and some of Mackintosh's ideas for the interior had to be dropped, although he did manage to retain the pillars decorated with blue and green tiles. The exterior is as unexpected as it is unique. We see recognisable elements of

design set in the hugely brave glass frontages of the two bold conical towers that stand either side of this building. Inside the towers the feeling of light, space and height on the stairways combined with the magical effect of those small colourful glass designs must have made made quite an impression on staff and pupils alike.

The school closed in 1979, though several years earlier rumours that the school was under threat of demolition began to spread. This was a difficult period for Glasgow. Regeneration had begun in the late sixties and with it came

the demolition of huge parts of the city. Many fine buildings were lost. In the 1970s HRH Princess Margaret visited the city and toured a number of Mackintosh buildings. It is widely believed that this visit saved Scotland Street School. Once closed as a school it became a museum dedicated to the history of education. Several period classrooms are on display as well as an exhibition area.

ABOVE LEFT
Scotland Street School

UPPER RIGHT
Interior staircase turret

LOWER RIGHT
Tiled pillars, first floor

house for an art lover

Designed by Charles Rennie Mackintosh in 1901 as a competition entry, the House for an Art Lover was built from the original drawings in the 1990s. It opened in 1996 housing a restaurant and exhibition space. It has become extremely popular and the setting in Bellahouston Park beside the Victorian walled garden has given the city a much used and attractive asset. True to its title, the house is often the venue for art exhibitions.

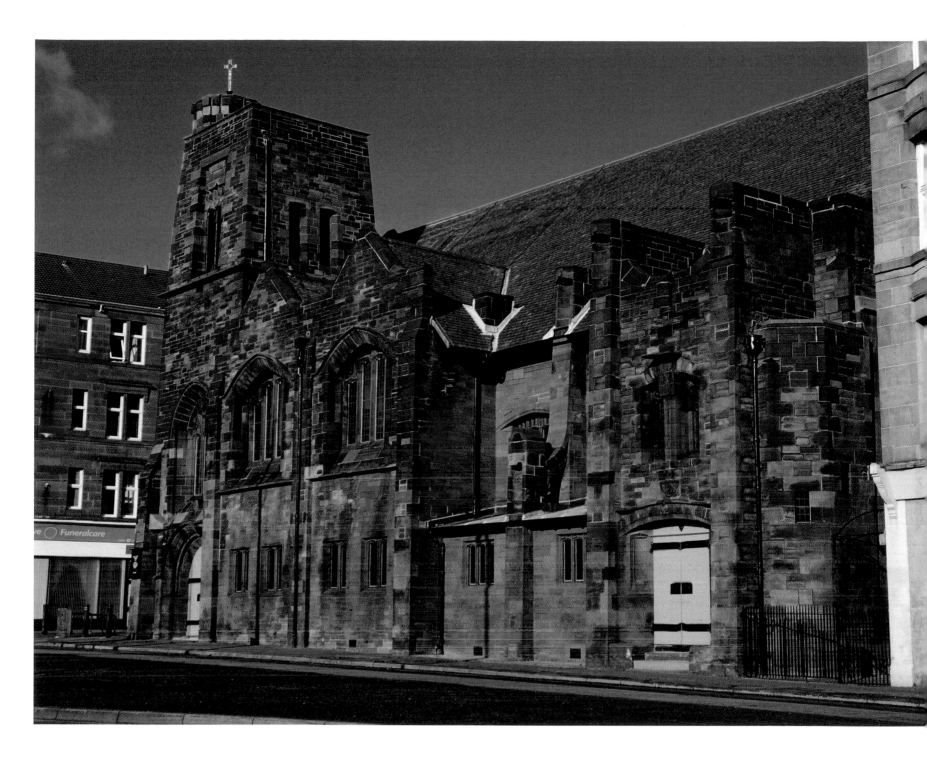

queen's cross church

Queen's Cross Church (1896–99) is the only church Mackintosh designed that was actually built. The site was quite restricted but Mackintosh made the most of it. Originally called St Matthew's Church it is known as Queen's Cross Church and is now the headquarters of the Charles Rennie Mackintosh Society.

It is the tower that is of special significance having been based on the tower of the Merriot Church in Somerset which he visited in 1895. Mackintosh had a genuine interest in the vernacular architecture of England.

These days, in front of the church on Garscube Road is a triangular traffic island whose mass of lampposts, CCTV cameras, traffic lights and signposts almost obscure this unique building.

art deco

After the First World War and the austerity that came with it there was a growing development within art and design, taking inspiration from styles old and new. Neoclassical, Cubism, Constructivism, Modernism, Art Nouveau, Bauhaus, Futurism, Aztec design and more.

This melded together to create an art movement called Art Deco which ran from 1925 to 1939. Essentially, Art Deco was a decorative movement and one which touched everything from household items such as radios through to cars, trains, ships and skyscrapers.

Cinemas, restaurants, houses, factories and an hotel were all built in and around Glasgow in the Art Deco style.

the beresford hotel
Built in 1938 to house visitors to the Empire Exhibition, the Beresford Hotel in Sauchiehall Street was the tallest building erected between the wars in Glasgow. During the Second World War it was a favourite haunt of American servicemen.

After the war it became an office block until 1964 when Strathclyde University took it over as student accomodation and renamed it Baird Hall.

In 2003 it was bought and converted into flats.

the luma lamp building
The Luma Lamp Factory was designed by Cornelius Armour and finished to coincide with the Empire Exhibition of 1938. This Art Deco building with its clean modernisitic lines has become something of a landmark being clearly visible from the nearby M8 motorway.

By the late seventies and early eighties the building had fallen into disrepair. In the nineties it was bought and converted into flats and brought back to life. It has won many awards since its conversion including the Europa Nostra Award in 1997.

LEFT
The Beresford Hotel building

RIGHT
The Luma Lamp building

rogano oyster bar

The Rogano Oyster Bar in Exchange Place is the oldest survivng restaurant in Glasgow and a truly iconic piece of architectural design.

It was opened in 1935 at the same time that the ocean liner the *Queen Mary* was being built on Clydeside by Cunard. The Art Deco interiors are the same as those on the *Queen Mary*. Rogano, being in the centre of the city, is a hugely popular bar and restaurant.

ABOVE LEFT
The restaurant

CENTRE LEFT and OPPOSITE
The champagne bar

BELOW LEFT
Sign in Exchange Place

botanic gardens

Glasgow is blessed with over ninety Council owned parks and several more gardens and stately homes owned by the National Trust for Scotland. Within the parks are several superb glasshouses, some in excellent condition, some derelict. There is also a wealth of sculpture, architecture and planting.

Kibble Palace is one of the largest glasshouses in the country. It underwent a major restoration which began in September 2003 reopening to the public in November 2006. During that time the entire building had been transported to South Yorkshire where the restoration work was carried out.

The glasshouse was originally given to the City of Glasgow and the Botanic Gardens in 1873 by John Kibble, who had it transported up the Clyde on a barge from its original home in Loch Long where it had been used as a conservatory at Kibble's home in Coulport. Once the barge arrived in Glasgow the glasshouse was carried on a cart to the Botanic Gardens.

The gardens themselves were established in 1839 to house the university's plant collection and to allow research. The collection was looked after by the Royal Botanic Society of Glasgow and when the gardens opened in 1842, public access was restricted to Saturdays and a charge was made.

In 1891 the burgh of Hillhead became part of Glasgow and the Botanic Gardens became one of the city's parks and were opened to the public free of charge. Kibble Palace is home to a number of marble sculptures as well as its magnificent plant collection. The centrepiece is the sculpture of Eve by Scipione Tadolini.

RIGHT
Statue of Eve in Kibble Palace

LEFT
Smaller glass dome, Kibble Palace

BELOW RIGHT
Kibble Palace

glasgow green

Glasgow Green is the oldest park in the city. Close to the city centre in the west, the cathedral in the north and the Clyde on its southern edge it is easy to see why this park is such a valuable asset for the people of Glasgow.

In its early days it was a far cry from the well tended park that it is today. The land was gifted in 1450 by James II to Bishop William Turnbull and the people of Glasgow as common land. It was a swampy area with uneven grounds and two burns running through it (the Molendinar and the Camlachie). It was also prone to flooding which was a fairly

common occurence. In the eighteenth century Glasgow expanded at a far faster rate than previously and this green area close to the centre of the town provided a much needed space which was used for a variety of purposes. Linen was dried and bleached in the sun, animals grazed and games were played. In the 1730s a wash house (steamie) was built which replaced the large outdoor tubs in which people washed their linens. The Green continued to be a centre for washing and drying into the twentieth century and a few of the old clothes poles still stand though some have been replaced.

In 1792 the park was extended with a gift from Patrick Bell of Cowcaddens of a piece of land to the east known as Fleshers' Haugh, an area of land upon which Bonny Prince Charlie's army had camped between 1745 and 1746.

Glasgow Green has seen a great many events and gatherings over the years. The Reform Act of 1832 brought a demonstration of over 70,000. The Suffragette Movement regularly held meetings from the 1870s. In 1917 workers walked to the Green to mark support for the Russian Revolution.

BELOW
Glasgow Green with the People's Palace and the Templeton Carpet Factory building

The St Andrew's Suspension Bridge (1855) which runs from Glasgow Green to Adelphi Street was built to replace a ferry that used to cross at that point carrying factory workers. It was, at times, a pretty dangerous crossing and a bridge was a far safer option. The bridge underwent a major overhaul in 1997.

Sitting close to the St Andrew's Suspension Bridge is Glasgow Humane Society House. The Society was formed in 1790 after the merchant James Coulter made a donation. At that time, with a lack of bridges, ferries were used to cross the river and many accidents occurred. The Society was formed to rescue those who were drowning and retrieve the bodies of those already drowned. Today the Humane Society, now a charity, still operates from the small boatyard on Glasgow Green under the watchful eye of George Parsonage MBE who took over from his late father Benjamin who had been the Society's officer since the thirties when the current house was built.

One of the Green's greatest assets is the People's Palace and Winter Gardens, which was built as a cultural centre. Opened by the Earl of Roseberry in 1898, it is now a museum solely concerned with the history of Glasgow. In front of the People's Palace sits the Doulton Fountain, which is the largest terracotta fountain in the world. It was built in 1888 at the Royal Doulton factory for the International Exhibition in Kelvingrove Park. After the exhibition the fountain was gifted to the city. In 2002 it was restored and reopened in 2005.

The last two weeks of July are the Glasgow Fair or Fair Fortnight, the Glasgow holiday, and a fairground is set up on the Green. The origins of the fair go back to 1190 when Bishop Jocelin and his successors were granted the right to a fair for eight days from July 7. For some time it was an important market selling horses and cattle amongst other things. Over time it developed and moved to the end of July. At one point it attracted a circus and theatres but eventually developed into the Glasgow Fair we have today which is more of a holiday than an event.

ABOVE
The Templeton Carpet Factory building (1889) now extended and renamed the Templeton Business Centre

RIGHT
Detail of window

OVERLEAF, LEFT
The Doulton Fountain (1888)

OVERLEAF, RIGHT
The Winter Garden of the People's Palace

ABOVE LEFT
St Andrew's Bridge and Glasgow
Humane Society House on
Glasgow Green

BELOW LEFT
St Andrew's Bridge and the
Glasgow Humane Society boatyard
from the River Clyde

RIGHT
The Glasgow Humane Society
boatyard

FAR RIGHT
Boat building in the Humane
Society boatyard

ABOVE
Nelson's Monument (1806),
Glasgow Green

RIGHT
Sir William Collins Memorial
Fountain (1881) and the
McLennan Arch (1843),
Glasgow Green

greenbank gardens

Greenbank House and Gardens has been a National Trust for Scotland property since 1976 when it was given to the Trust by Mr and Mrs W.P. Blyth who were responsible for the ornamental planting which gives the garden its unique feel. Individual areas have been created by the use of hedges and tall plants giving scope for sculptures and water features as well as a wide variety of plants.

Greenbank House and Gardens were established in 1763 by Robert Allason, a Glasgow merchant, as a country retreat. He purchased the land from Flenders Farm which at one time had been in his family.

The garden itself is split into a series of themed gardens. In the foam garden the bronze water nymph in the centre of the water feature was originally sculpted for the 1938 Empire Exhibition. In 1988 it was lent to the Glasgow Garden Festival.

UPPER RIGHT
Greenbank House from the garden

LOWER RIGHT
Greenbank House front courtyard

OPPOSITE
Water nymph in the foam garden

pollok country park and house

Voted Europe's Best Park in 2008 and Best Park in Britain in 2007, Pollok Country Park is the gem of the south side, and the largest park in the city. In 1967 Mrs Anne Maxwell Macdonald and family gifted the house and 360 acres of the estate to the City Council on the condition that it remained a public park.

The estate was the ancestral home of the Maxwell family for over 700 years and several houses had been built over the years. The present house was designed by William Adam and was completed in 1752. Extensions were added in the years leading up to 1908.

The country park and grounds are cared for by the Council but the house itself is managed by the National Trust for Scotland and contains an excellent collection of paintings, furniture, glassware and silver.

The gardens close to the house tend to be formal and are beautifully laid out. There is a good collection of rhododendrons and much woodland. Many paths and walks run through the

BELOW
Pollok House, the National Trust for Scotland

OPPOSITE
Pollok House gardens

grounds. There is also a golf course and allotments. Nearby the house are the old stables and estate management buildings as well as a sawmill which was operated using the waters of the River Cart which flows through the estate. At one time the sawmill was used to generate electricity and provided power for the house.

the burrell collection

When the shipping magnate, philanthropist and art collector Sir William Burrell (1861–1958) gifted his lifetimes collection to the City of Glasgow in 1944 it was on the condition that it was to be housed 16 miles from the centre of the city to avoid air pollution and any resulting damage to the collection. By the time Sir William Burrell died in 1958 the collection still had no home and it was not until the Maxwell Family gifted Pollok Estate in 1967 that the city had a suitable site for the building of a museum. The Burrell was the result of an architectural competition held in the early 1970s. The building was opened by Queen Elizabeth II in 1983.

The collection itself is wide ranging and has over 8,000 items. Collected during a lifetime of travel it includes complete stone doorways, paintings, ceramics, tapestries, stained glass, sculpture, medieval weapons and armour, furniture, ancient Egyptian artefacts, Islamic art, Chinese artefacts and more. It is an astonishing collection held in a remarkable building and one of the city's highlights. The setting in Pollok Park allows the buildings use of glass to give the feel of being a part of the landscape whilst at the same time allowing light to filter through the trees and enhance the exhibits.

LEFT
The Burrell

ABOVE RIGHT
The museum interior melds with the landscape

BELOW RIGHT
Museum interior

OPPOSITE ABOVE
Stained glass detail in the restaurant

OPPOSITE BELOW
Stained glass display

ABOVE RIGHT
The Warwick Vase and sculptures share a quiet space

BELOW RIGHT
Sixteenth century portal and door, Hornby Castle

kelvingrove park

Designed by Sir Joseph Paxton on land purchased between 1852 and 1854, this is a fine example of a Victorian park. There was a real need for areas of open space at the time because of rapid urban growth and the problems that came with it. The laying out of the park took fifteen years and it was so well received that Paxton was given two further commissions: Queen's Park and Alexandria Park.

He had previously designed the Botanic Gardens in Glasgow as well as the Crystal Palace in London.

Kelvingrove Park has hosted two International Exhibitions in 1888 and 1901 as well as the Scottish National Exhibition in 1911.

There are several fine sculptures and monuments in the park. The Stewart Memorial Fountain (1872) commemorates Lord Provost Stewart of Murdostoun who was involved in the creation of the first fresh water supply to Glasgow from Loch Katrine. From the late eighteenth century the waters of the River Clyde had become overused and polluted giving rise to cholera and typhoid epidemics. Public health became a major issue and finding a fresh water supply was central to that.

The Highland Light Infantry Monument dates from 1906 and commemorates the men who fell in the Boer War. The sculptor was William Birnie Rhind.

The Monument to Lord Frederick Sleigh Roberts, V.C. was built in 1916 by public subscription. Lord Roberts was a career soldier who fought in the many colonial wars during Queen Victoria's reign. He distinguished himself on several ocasions becoming one of the greatest heroes of the time. Awarded the Victoria Cross at the age of twenty-six for his gallantry during the Indian Mutiny, he eventually became the head of the armed services. During the First World War he died in the retreat from Marne. He was in his eighties.

RIGHT
Monument to Lord Frederick
Sleigh Roberts

LEFT
The Stewart Memorial Fountain

LEFT
The Highland Light Infantry
Monument, Kelvingrove Park

RIGHT
Kelvingrove Art Gallery and
Museum

OVERLEAF, CLOCKWISE FROM
TOP
Kelvingrove Art Gallery and
Museum interior

Kelvingrove Art Gallery and
Museum exterior

Museum interior with spitfire

kelvingrove art gallery and museum

Built in the grounds of the now demolished Kelvingrove House, Kelvingrove Art Gallery and Museum was conceived out of the necessity to find a home for the city's municipal collections which, throughout the latter half of the nineteenth century, found themselves being housed between the McLellan Galleries and Kelvingrove House itself. The grounds had been purchased by the city in 1852 and Kelvingrove House (designed by Robert Adam) turned into a museum.

Profits from the success of the 1888 exhibition held in Kelvingrove Park (known then as West End Park) allowed the city to make plans to build a permanent home. Extra funds were raised through private subscription. Once funding was secured, an architectural competition took place in two stages and was won by architects John W. Simpson and E.J. Milner Allen. There was some controversy at the time as they were London based and many thought that a Glasgow firm should have been chosen.

Such had been the success of the 1888 exhibition that another was planned to inaugurate the Art Gallery and Museum in 1901. This too was a huge success with over 11 million visitors and the profits were used to both restore the park and give a much needed boost to the Art Purchase Fund for the gallery.

The Kelvingrove Art Gallery and Museum is the most visited museum in Scotland. A three year restoration programme costing £27.9 million ran from 2003 and Kelvingrove was reopened by the Queen on July 11, 2006.

Many of the exhibits are now interactive and the mix of exhibiting styles is proving extremely popular.

queen's park

Situated on the site of the Battle of Langside (1568) and dedicated to Mary Queen of Scots (who was defeated), Queen's Park was designed by Sir Joseph Paxton in 1860.

The park is in the south of the city close to the Victoria Infirmary and at its southern end is the memorial to the Battle of Langside.

Not all of Paxton's ideas were used when the park was built though there is fine example of a glasshouse which has within it a collection of cacti and succulents, a pond and a café.

When Glasgow expanded its boundaries in 1890, Queen's Park fell within the city. In 1894 the city puchased the neighbouring estate of Camphill on the western edge of the park and incorporated it into the park as a whole. Thus, Queen's Park became of some considerable size and this created a valuable and much used green space in the Langside and Strathbungo area.

The park also contains two ponds and an impressive set of steps.

ABOVE
Winter Garden dome, Queen's Park

LEFT
Gateway to Winter Garden glasshouse

victoria park

Victoria Park was named after Queen Victoria in 1886 which was the year of her Golden Jubilee. The park is located in the west of the city close to the northern entrance of the Clyde Tunnel. The Park is a valuable asset in this busy resedential area and has many attrcations including the Fossil Grove containing fossilised trees discovered when the park was built.

There is an open area for football which is used by the Scottish Australian Rules Football League.

Hidden in the yard area which contains the offices and storage for the Council, there is a small purpose built curling club (1901) and outdoor rink. Owned by the Partick Curling Club, it relies on there being winters cold enough to freeze the rink.

TOP LEFT
Four dial miniature lamppost clock

TOP RIGHT
War memorial

BELOW LEFT
Partick Curling Club

springburn park

ABOVE LEFT
The derelict Winter Gardens

ABOVE RIGHT
The unicorn (1912), the upper part
of the Balgray Fountain

Renowned for its diversity of wildlife, part of Springburn Park has been designated as a Site of Importance for Nature Conservation.

The park has both ponds and, in the centre, the Cockmuir Reservoirs which supply water to large areas of northern Glasgow.

There are several interesting highlights including a rather wonderful rockery and a garden of peace. The now derelict Winter Gardens were in good condition in the seventies but suffered vandalism and have been left to deteriorate. An A listed building, they were built as part of a gift to Springburn from Hugh Reid of the North British Locomotive Company.

The white terracotta column topped with the unicorn is part of the Balgray Fountain by Royal Doulton which once stood in the now non-existent Balgray Leisure Park. It was dismantled in the early seventies and brought to Springburn but sadly only the upper part of the fountain was reconstructed.

The land, which had been owned by Glasgow Corporation since 1892 was extended in 1900 when Hugh Reid bought the lands of Cockmuir and presented them to the city.

hampden park

In a city that has four senior football clubs including Rangers FC (Ibrox) and Celtic FC (Celtic Park), Hampden holds a special place not only in Glasgow's heart but across the world. It is a truly iconic stadium.

Hampden is home to Queens Park FC and, as Scotland's National Stadium, home to Scotland's national football team. The Scottish Cup Final is played here annually in May and many international games are hosted. Hampden also provides a venue for other sporting events such as rugby and American football. Indeed, for three years between 1969 and 1972 it was the home of the Glasgow Tigers Speedway team. The Rolling Stones have played Hampden as have Rod Stewart, Robbie Williams, the Eagles, the Red Hot Chili Peppers and many more.

On top of all that the stadium houses the offices of the Scottish Football League and the Scottish Football Association.

Queens Park Football Club built Hampden on land purchased in 1903 and they built the biggest and most technically advanced stadium in the world which paid off immediately when Hampden was quickly adopted as Scotland's National Stadium. Hampden remained the world's largest stadium until the 1950s.

In the 1990s the formation of the National Stadium Committee gave the impetus needed to raise funding for the first phase of the much needed refurbishment which involved upgrading the north and east stands as well as providing hospitality lounges, car parking and improving landscaping.

Rebuilding the south stand and redeveloping the west stand came next and the work was completed in May 1999.

LEFT
Hampden Park Stadium

regeneration

The regeneration process that Glasgow is currently undergoing began prior to the Second World War during the economic depression left in the wake of the First World War, a downturn which stretched into the 1930s. To give confidence to the city and to demonstrate a bright new future, Glasgow hosted the Empire Exhibition in 1938 in Bellahouston Park.

The Second World War erupted soon afterwards and although the cry for arms and military equipment gave heavy industry in Glasgow a great deal of work, the city fathers were aware that once the war was over the need for regeneration would be their focus.

Glasgow Corporation (the then governing body) commissioned two reports. The First Planning Report, published in March 1945, and the Clyde Valley Regional Plan. These reports were written by Corporation engineer Robert Bruce and have become known as the Bruce Report. The main thrust of the reports were a series of initiatives which were to completely change the city over a fifty year period. Only a part of the report was sanctioned.

The city centre, by merit of its importance, was the prime target of change. It was proposed that much of the centre should be demolished to make way for a new architectural approach (the Victorian style was perceived as being old fashioned). The redevelopment of the centre included redesigning the rail system with the creation of a Glasgow North Station in the Buchanan Street area and a Glasgow South Station on the site of Central Station. The idea was to rebuild the majority of the city centre to a single plan based on the formality of the new architecture of the time. By not sanctioning this section of the report, Glasgow retained what has become one of the great city centres.

Part of the report recommended that much of the population of the city (which numbered almost 1.5 million) should be moved to new housing developments at the edge of the city.

The main focus was on areas that were overcrowded and had become slums. The idea was to both lessen the burden on the city itself and to offer a new fresh start for those being moved.

This part of the report was carried out almost in full although many people were moved outside of the city boundaries. In the 1950s nearly 750,000 people were relocated. New urban housing schemes were developed in areas like Castlemilk, Priesthill, Easterhouse and Drumchapel. The new towns of East Kilbride and Cumbernauld were created.

This greatly affected the population of inner city Glasgow which currently stands at approximately 600,000.

As part of the transport policy, the Bruce Report also recommended the creation of a series of motorways which would meet to create an inner ring road. Work began in the sixties with the M8 motorway and the construction of the Kingston Bridge. The motorway carved a path straight through the city just west of its centre.

The process caused much controversy and the inner ring road plan was dropped. Fifty years on work has begun on linking the M8 to the M74 through the south side of the city though not through part of Glasgow Green as the Bruce Report had advocated. Archeological digs have been taking place on parts of the motorway route to rescue as much historical data as possible before building begins in earnest.

Since the 1980s the regeneration programme has been fairly wide ranging and regeneration in itself is a very different animal than it was even seventy years ago when wholesale demolition was thought to be the answer. These days a much more considered approach is put into play taking into consideration individual communities and buildings and putting into place the building blocks to encourage enterprise, create business and provide both work and recreational pursuits.

RIGHT
Statue of Scotland's first First Minister, Donald Dewar, in front of the Royal Glasgow Concert Hall in Buchanan Street

LEFT and RIGHT
Red Road flats

ABOVE
Flats by the Clyde and the Albert Bridge

ABOVE RIGHT
Christmas shoppers in Buchanan Street

BELOW RIGHT
Looking toward the City Chambers from Port Dundas

ABOVE
The Mitchell Library with the M8 motorway in front. The Mitchell Library is Europe's largest public reference library

LEFT
The South Portland Street Bridge was built between 1851 and 1853 and the two stone arches are the oldest surviving segments of bridge on the Clyde within Glasgow. More than two thousand LED lights are used to illuminate the bridge at night

RIGHT and BELOW
The *Waverley* at Pacific Quay

OPPOSITE
Dry dock area at the end of Princes Dock

the river

The riverside has been the focus of attention since the eighties. The stretch of river that runs through Glasgow is known as the Clyde Corridor with the area where the Kelvin flows into the Clyde known as Glasgow Harbour. Glasgow Harbour is the single largest development on the river since the Pacific Quay regeneration which began over twenty years ago and which is still ongoing. Several miles of works on both banks range from homes to businesses and recreational areas. The river has been the focus of life for over a thousand years and the plan is to make available areas of riverside which have been locked away behind docks and shipyard walls for many decades. Old warehouse and dockside areas have been opened up. New housing has been constructed and work has begun on the Riverside Museum at Pointhouse Quay designed by Zaha Hadid. Walkways will mean that almost the whole frontage will be accessible for the first time in many decades and the increase in the number of footbridges around Pacific Quay gives easy access to both sides of the river.

Plans have been made to increase use of the river itself. There is a pontoon at the Broomielaw Quay and other pontoons are being planned which hopefully will attract river traffic and allow new water bus services to be introduced. The paddle steamer *Waverley* berthed at Princes Dock operates a leisure cruise service for periods of the summer and over winters in Glasgow at the Princes dock end of Pacific Quay.

The *Waverley* was built just after the war by Harland and Wolf for the London and North Eastern Railway Company. Launched in 1947, the *Waverley* was specifically built to operate from the Clyde. Over the years she was well looked after by her various owners but in 1973 faced the prospect of becoming a museum piece. The Paddle Steamer Preservation Society bought her for £1 and saved her from that fate with the help of grants from both Glasgow Corporation and Strathclyde Region and more recently the Lottery. These days the *Waverley* is regularly seen on the Firth of Clyde and often ventures further afield.

LEFT
The Science Centre and the
Glasgow Tower

ABOVE
The Science Centre and Imax
Cinema from the Glasgow Tower

princes dock

On the south side of the river opposite Queens Dock was
Plantation Quay which had been completed in 1874. The
fifteenth Clyde Trust Act passed in 1883 authorised the
construction of two new docks. One near the west end of
the Plantation Quay wall and the other near Whitefield Road,
Govan. This huge dock area was to be known as Princes
Dock (later to become part of the greater Pacific Quay) and
was built in sections supported by concrete cylinders and
finished in masonry, the first being open to shipping in 1892
and the last in 1897. It had an outer basin 1,150 feet in length
and a width ranging from 505 to 676 feet and three inner
basins of differing lengths, the longest being 1,528 feet. The
outer basin has a depth that varies from 20 feet to 28 feet at
low water. A steam crane capable of loads of 130 tons was
constructed at the deepest end of the quay.

In 1903 Princes Dock was given a rail link known as

the Princes Dock Joint Railway. The link was a siding from the Glasgow to Govan line. It was jointly owned by the Caledonian Railway, Glasgow and South Railway and North British Railway. The line was eventually lifted in 1970 after being out of service for some time.

In 1988 a National Garden Festival was held on Pacific Quay and Princes Dock played its part. This was the third of five national garden festivals and ran from April until September bringing hundreds of thousands of visitors to the city.

The preparations were extensive with top soil being dredged from the river and nurseries across Scotland supplying trees, shrubs and plants. A new footbridge, Bell's Bridge, connected the festival site to the north bank. There were several themed areas such as 'science and technology', health and well-being', 'water and maritime', 'a Victorian street' and 'recreation and sport'. A narrow gauge railway called the

Festival Railway Line ran through the site.

On show too were examples of the housing that would be built on parts of the site and the north bank when the Festival ended.

After the Festival, much of the site including Princes Dock lay derelict for several years. In the late nineties construction began on the Glasgow Science Centre, Imax Cinema and the Millennium Tower (later to become the Glasgow Tower).

The Imax Cinema opened first in October 2000 and is the only Imax cinema in Scotland.

The Tower and Science centre opened in 2001.

The Tower stands at 127 metres and is the tallest structure in Scotland though it does not qualify as a building. There is a viewing platform at 105 metres. It is built in the shape of an aeroplane wing and computer controlled motors turn it into the wind to reduce resistance.

ABOVE
Cranes on the George V Dock

RIGHT
View across the Barclay, Curle &
Co Ltd yard